Dear Parent:

Congratulations! Your child is taking the first steps on an exciting journey. The destination? Independent reading!

STEP INTO READING® will help your child get there. The program offers books at five levels that accompany children from their first attempts at reading to reading success. Each step includes fun stories, fiction and nonfiction, and colorful art. There are also Step into Reading Sticker Books, Step into Reading Math Readers, Step into Reading Write-In Readers, Step into Reading Phonics Readers, and Step into Reading Phonics First Steps! Boxed Sets—a complete literacy program with something to interest every child.

Learning to Read, Step by Step!

Ready to Read   Preschool–Kindergarten
• big type and easy words • rhyme and rhythm • picture clues
For children who know the alphabet and are eager to begin reading.

Reading with Help   Preschool–Grade 1
• basic vocabulary • short sentences • simple stories
For children who recognize familiar words and sound out new words with help.

Reading on Your Own   Grades 1–3
• engaging characters • easy-to-follow plots • popular topics
For children who are ready to read on their own.

Reading Paragraphs   Grades 2–3
• challenging vocabulary • short paragraphs • exciting stories
For newly independent readers who read simple sentences with confidence.

Ready for Chapters   Grades 2–4
• chapters • longer paragraphs • full-color art
For children who want to take the plunge into chapter books but still like colorful pictures.

STEP INTO READING® is designed to give every child a successful reading experience. The grade levels are only guides. Children can progress through the steps at their own speed, developing confidence in their reading, no matter what their grade.

Remember, a lifetime love of reading starts with a single step!

The publisher would like to thank Rear Admiral W. J. Holland, Jr., USN (RET), for his invaluable assistance in the preparation of this book.

Cover photograph: The Stocktrek Corp./Getty Images.
Interior photographs: page 3: U.S. Navy photograph by Chief Yeoman Alphonso Braggs; pages 5 and 21: Defense Visual Information Center at March ARB, CA; page 6: courtesy of General Dynamics Electric Boat; page 7: photograph by Bill Curtsinger/National Geographic; page 8: U.S. Navy photograph; page 9: U.S. Department of Defense graphic by Ron Stern; pages 12, 36, and 47: U.S. Navy photograph by Photographer's Mate 1st Class David A. Levy; page 13: U.S. Navy photograph by Photographer's Mate 2nd Class Jeffrey S. Viano; pages 14–15, 17, 29, and 38: U.S. Naval Historical Center photographs; pages 19 and 43: © Yogi Kaufman; page 20: U.S. Navy photograph by Chief Photographer's Mate John E. Gay; page 22: U.S. Navy photograph by Photographer's Mate 1st Class David C. Lloyd; page 27: *K-19: The Widowmaker* © Paramount Pictures, all rights reserved; page 28: Hulton-Deutsch Collection/CORBIS; page 30: U.S. Navy photograph by Photographer's Mate 1st Class Kevin H. Tierney; pages 32 and 45: courtesy of U.S. Navy Art Collection; pages 33 (top and bottom), 34, 37, and 46: © Steve Kaufman; page 35: U.S. Navy photograph, now in the collections of the National Archives; page 39: NavSource photograph courtesy of John J. Cook (www.navsource.org); pages 40 and 41: AP/Wide World Photos; page 42: © Smithsonian Institution, NMAH-Transportation; page 44: U.S. Navy photograph by Photographer's Mate Airman Rob Gaston; page 48: photograph by Steve Kaufman/CORBIS.

www.stepintoreading.com

Educators and librarians, for a variety of teaching tools, visit us at www.randomhouse.com/teachers

Library of Congress Cataloging-in-Publication Data
Kramer, Sydelle.
Submarines / by S. A. Kramer. — 1st ed.
  p. cm. — (Step into reading. A step 4 book)
ISBN 0-375-82574-6 (trade) — ISBN 0-375-92574-0 (lib. bdg.)
1. Submarines (Ships)—Juvenile literature.
I. Title. II. Series: Step into reading. Step 4 book.
VM365.K73 2005 623.825'7—dc22 2004014239

Printed in the United States of America First Edition 10 9 8 7 6 5 4 3 2 1

STEP INTO READING, RANDOM HOUSE, and the Random House colophon are registered trademarks of Random House, Inc.

(opposite page) Three polar bears approach the attack submarine USS *Honolulu,* surfaced 280 miles from the North Pole.

STEP INTO READING

STEP 4

SUBMARINES

by S. A. Kramer

— with photographs —

Random House 🏠 New York

Introduction

The Voyage Begins

Up the gangplank, into the submarine! Ready for the most dangerous trip of your life?

Deep beneath the waves, there's no day or night, no newspapers, radio, or TV. You and the crew will be cut off from the world.

The voyage may last for months. You'll work, sleep, then work some more. You'll never totally relax. For disaster can strike at any time, sending a sub to the bottom.

The tiniest leak can become a flood. A fire may rage out of control. You could collide with another boat or an underwater mountain. If the power fails, poisonous gases will fill the air.

Yet submariners love their work! They search for enemy ships or spy on unfriendly countries. By studying the ocean, they serve science. And if there's a war, they fight from secret underwater locations.

It's time to go!

"Dive!" the captain orders. The deck tilts, then gets steeper. You fling your arms around a pole.

Whoosh. The sub makes strange groaning sounds.

On to the unknown!

Chapter I

Into the Deep

You're aboard a nuclear submarine—
a sub that runs on nuclear power. It's the
deadliest fighting machine ever built. The
most complicated and expensive, too. Its
mission is so top-secret, not everyone on
board knows where it's going.

Today all of America's subs are nuclear-powered. There are two kinds: ballistic missile and attack. A ballistic missile sub is larger—560 feet, or nearly two football fields long. Its nuclear missiles can strike at a moment's notice.

Illustration of ballistic missile submarine USS *Ohio*.

Conceptual drawing of *Virginia*-class attack submarine.

An attack sub is smaller. It battles enemy subs, spies on foreign shores, and lays mines in harbors. Among its weapons are torpedoes and missiles.

It's amazing that such powerful ships are made to sink on purpose! To dive, a sub replaces air in special tanks on board with seawater. The tanks are called ballast tanks, and the seawater becomes ballast.

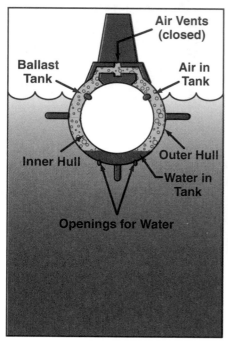

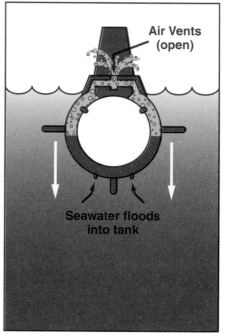

SURFACED   **SUBMERGING**

When a submarine is at the surface, its ballast tanks are mostly full of air. To submerge, air vents at the top of the tanks are opened. Seawater then floods into the tanks from openings in the bottom. This rising water forces the air up and out of the vents. This causes the submarine to start sinking.

The crew regulates ballast by opening vents at the top of the tanks. The vents allow air to shoot out. Openings at the bottom let water in. Water is heavy. Down goes the sub.

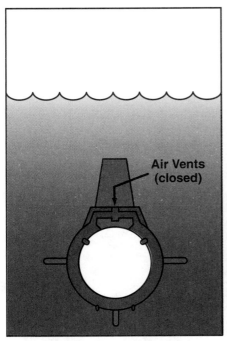

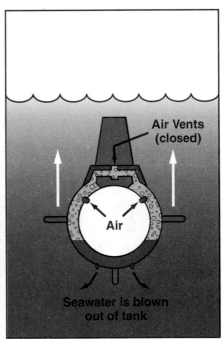

SUBMERGED   **SURFACING**

When the ballast tanks are full of water, the submarine is submerged, or fully beneath the surface of the water. To make the submarine rise to the surface again, compressed air is blown into the tanks from inside the submarine. This forces the water out of the openings on the bottom and causes the submarine to rise.

Your sub is stopping at periscope depth—60 feet under. A periscope is a long tube fitted with mirrors. It is used to see above the water's surface. If the sub is below 60 feet, the periscope won't work.

You and the crew check to make sure it's safe to keep diving. All equipment must be stored away or held down. If there's a sudden turn or dive, loose objects will go flying.

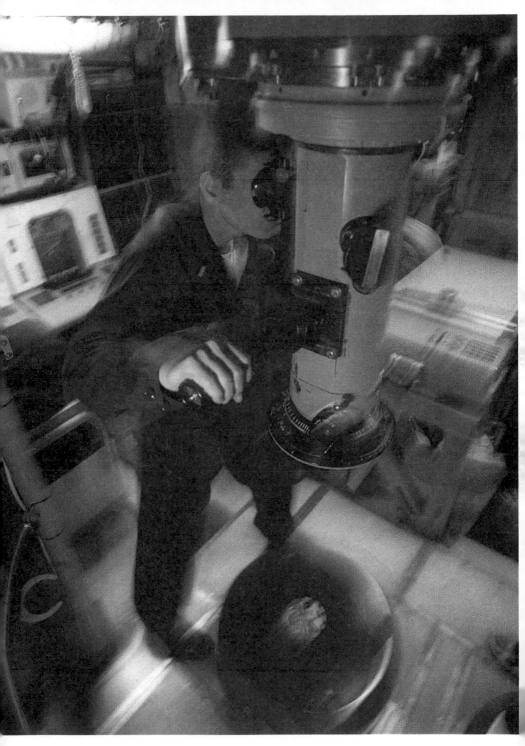

A sailor searches for surface ships with a periscope.

You also check for leaks. These can result from a broken part or a sailor's mistake. Submarines have sunk because the wrong valve was opened or was never closed.

Here's an example. In 1920, someone forgot to shut a main valve on the *S-5*, a U.S. submarine. When it started to dive,

U.S. submarine *S-5*, 1920.

some compartments flooded. Down went the sub, 180 feet. It rammed nose-first into deep mud.

Most of the crew escaped the flooded compartments. Still, they weren't safe—the sub would soon run out of air. To survive, they had to reach the surface.

Sailors blew air into the ballast tanks to make the sub rise. But the *S-5*'s buried nose didn't budge. Instead, its rear end tipped up, straight out of the sea! There was no escape from the rear. The crew was desperate. So some sailors climbed to the rear. Drilling holes in the sub's body, they jammed a pipe out into the air. On it flew a white T-shirt. Would anyone see it?

Two ships did. Their men made a big hole in the sub where it rose from the water. Out scrambled the crew. It was a miraculous rescue!

Your sub has no leaks. Now you head for test depth—the deepest a sub can safely go.

The stern (rear) of the *S-5* showing above water
after it sank on September 1, 1920.

Water is heavy and puts pressure on a sub's hull, or body. This body is made of two parts, one inside the other. The inner hull, called the pressure hull, is made of thick steel plates. At test depth, these plates are strong enough to keep out the sea.

But as a sub dives deeper, it reaches a point below which the sea becomes stronger. Sailors call that crush depth. Below crush depth, a sub caves in like an empty soda can.

But your sub is safe. It's swimming so easily, you can't tell you're moving. A sub underwater glides as effortlessly as a fish.

Ready? Let's take a look around.

Chapter II

Inside the Fighting Machine

You step down walkways no wider than a man, squeezing through two-foot-wide hatches. Everywhere you go, there are dials and switches, buttons and gauges. Pipes cover the walls, called bulkheads.

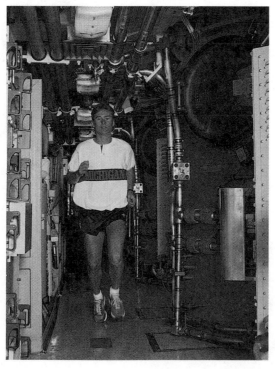

A sailor keeps fit on patrol. Twelve laps around the missile compartment equal one mile.

Now you reach the attack center. The size of a bedroom, it's the underwater command center. Here the sub is steered, weapons fired, and periscopes raised.

A sailor operates the main control aboard the nuclear-powered submarine USS *Seawolf*.

A Tomahawk cruise missile launched from the submarine USS *Florida*.

Next comes the sonar shack, no bigger than a closet. Four men are crammed inside. Sonar listens for noises and can send out sound waves to locate objects underwater.

These sound waves bounce off whatever lurks out there and then bounce back to tell you where the objects are. Sonar can "hear" everything from passing ships to whales. It allows you to track an enemy sub without giving away your location.

Sonar station on board the USS *Toledo* nuclear-powered attack submarine.

There are two types of sonar:

PASSIVE SONAR listens for noises using electronic listening equipment.

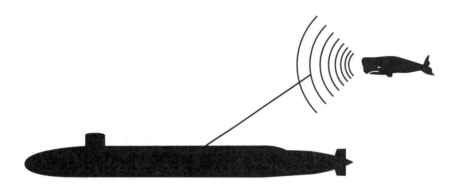

ACTIVE SONAR sends out sound waves, which bounce back when they hit an object.

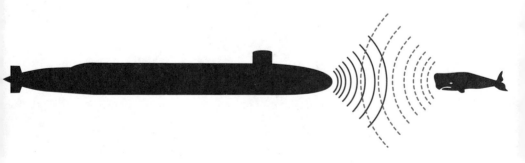

Now you've arrived at the nuclear reactor. This device powers the sub.

The reactor heats water to make steam to run the engine and to make electricity. This power turns seawater into oxygen to breathe and water to drink. It also gets rid of carbon dioxide, a gas that can kill people if it fills the air.

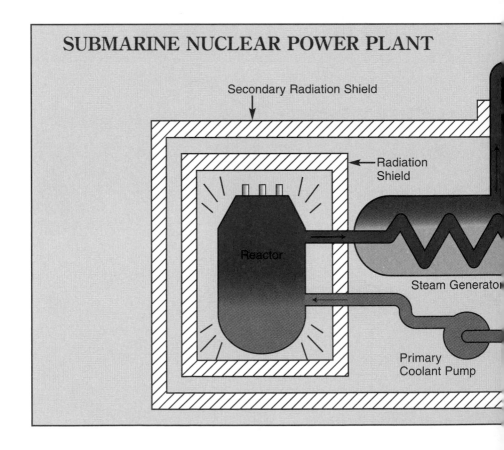

SUBMARINE NUCLEAR POWER PLANT

Secondary Radiation Shield

Radiation Shield

Reactor

Steam Generator

Primary Coolant Pump

You notice a heavy shield surrounding the reactor. It's there because when the reactor creates energy, it releases deadly rays called radiation. Here's what can happen if radiation escapes from the shield, or if people have to go inside it.

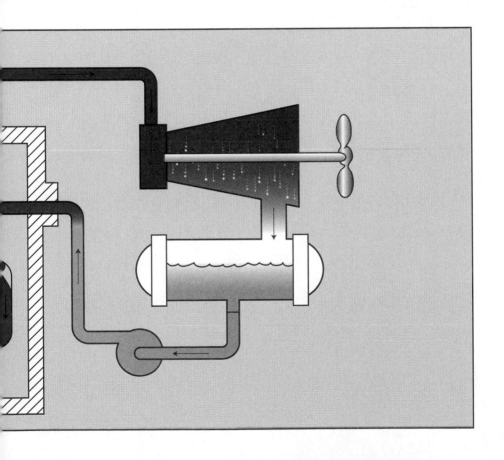

In 1961, the reactor on *K-19*, a Russian sub, began to fail. The crew watched in horror as it heated up way past normal to 1,470 degrees. If the temperature continued to rise, the reactor could melt. Then there would be a terrible explosion. The sub would be doomed.

The crew knew it had to prevent disaster. But the only way to do that was to open the shield. Whoever did would be poisoned by radiation. Plus, the deadly rays would seep through the sub, making everyone sick. Eight brave men opened the shield to fix the reactor. The temperature went down—but the men soon died. The captain and some other crew members eventually died, too. Yet the sub and the rest of the crew were saved.

The plot of the movie *K-19: The Widowmaker* was inspired by the actual events that took place on the Russian submarine *K-19*.

Nuclear reactors can be dangerous—but they also make running subs easy. Before subs started using nuclear power in 1954, they needed two different engines. One used diesel fuel and drove the sub on the surface. The second used batteries and drove the sub underwater.

The crew of a U.S. Navy submarine, March 1917.

The USS *Shark* (left) and the USS *Porpoise* (right) on cradles at the New York Navy Yard, circa 1905.

But the batteries didn't last long. Every night a sub had to surface to recharge them. In wartime, planes and ships would spot the subs and destroy them.

Before nuclear power, subs couldn't dive deeper than 450 feet. The air inside was cold and stunk of fuel. Subs were called pigboats.

Today machinery keeps the air on board clean and comfortable. Subs can stay underwater several months. And some can dive over half a mile down.

It's a different world under the waves. What's a submariner's life really like?

Chapter III

Below

Living underwater is a big challenge. The Navy doesn't want its men doing it all the time. It gets too hard after a while. Why?

You never see your loved ones—in fact, you can't even call or write. Sometimes there's e-mail, but usually they're in touch only through a "familygram"—a note that's just 40 words long.

```
USS MEMPHIS
030418ZOCT04
FAMILYGRAM
FOR MM1 THOMAS DALY
FALL'S ARRIVED. FLOWERS BLOOMING. TOMMY
ALL A'S. SHEILA SINGING IN SCHOOL MUSICAL.
FIONA STARTING TO WALK. THANKSGIVING AT
MOTHER'S WITH ALL. MISS YOU DEAREST. LOVE.
ANNE
```

Then there's the boredom. On a sub, every day seems the same. You do the job you've been trained for, then clean, make repairs, or stand watch. There's constant drilling for war or emergencies. There's some time to read or watch movies or train for new jobs, and about six hours to sleep.

All Hands Below by Georges Schreiber, watercolor, 1943. Crewmen on board a U.S. Navy submarine play a round of cards to relieve the tension of hours spent underwater.

Sailors load supplies on board the USS *San Francisco*.

Inspecting a torpedo tube.

Or at least *try* to sleep. A drill can be called at any time. Plus, your bed isn't very comfortable. It's a short, narrow bunk called a rack. Stacked in threes, racks are so close to one another that there's barely enough room for you to roll over.

Crewman reading in his bunk, circa 1987.

Racks can be anywhere—next to a machine, a torpedo, even a nuclear missile! If you're really unlucky, your rack may stick out into the passageway, and sailors step on it as they pass. Or you may have to share your rack with someone else—he sleeps during one shift, you sleep during another. This is called "hot bunking."

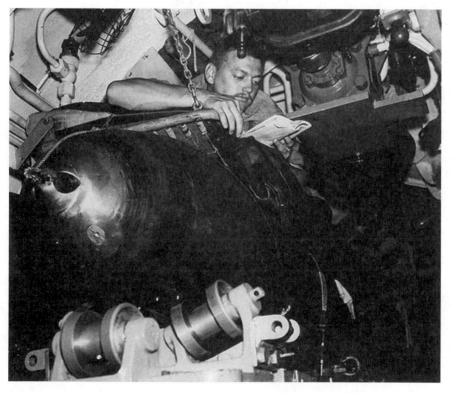

Crewman reading in his bunk (atop a torpedo!), circa 1945.

No wonder the crew is often tired. But that doesn't mean you can slack off.

Working together as a team, submariners stay constantly on the alert. Your life—and the lives of everyone on board—depends on it.

A commanding officer observes the action in the control room during a hot-run toxic gas drill.

Sailors handle lines at an explosives-handling wharf in Bangor,
Washington.

The USS *Thresher* at sea on July 24, 1961.

Still, accidents happen. In 1963, the USS *Thresher* went for a test dive and never came up. A leaky pipe damaged the electrical system, and the nuclear reactor shut down. The sub went into an uncontrollable dive and broke into little pieces. Every man died.

Accidents happen to weapons on board, too. In 2000, a torpedo misfired on board the Russian nuclear sub *Kursk*. That set off a reaction that sparked an explosion so huge, it blew a hole through the hull. Plunging to the bottom, the sub was doomed. Yet amazingly, a handful of men survived the explosion. Praying for help, they lived for hours in the cold and dark. As they breathed in poisonous fumes, they wrote farewell notes to their families. Stormy seas made their rescue impossible, and eventually, they died, too.

Crew members of the Russian submarine *Kursk* stand on the ship's deck during a naval parade on July 30, 2000.

A moment of silence is observed in Moscow, August 12, 2002, during the unveiling of a monument to the sailors who died on the submarine *Kursk*.

Yet it's not just the threat of death that makes submarine life hard. What's easy to do on land can be far more difficult underwater.

Need to use the bathroom? Here, it's called the head. It's not like the one at home—it's small and tight. Let's hope you're not in a rush. There are only six toilets and four showers for close to 140 men.

Hungry? Head for the cafeteria, called the mess. At first, there's plenty of fresh food. But after two weeks or so, only frozen, powdered, or canned goods are served. Ice cream, however, is always available!

Signed up for the military? Doesn't matter if you're a boy or a girl—unless you want to serve on a sub. Women aren't allowed. The Navy has strict rules against mixing the sexes in such close quarters.

But the hardships of life on board are far from your thoughts now. Your sub is almost home.

Chapter IV

The Voyage Ends

Up the sub goes! Surfacing is noisy. Air
blasts into the ballast tanks, pushing
seawater out. The hull pops as the weight
of water lessens. Suddenly it's quiet—
you're at the top!

Up the Hatch by Thomas Hart Benton, oil on pressboard, circa 1944. Crewmen of a U.S. submarine race up ladders to get through the open hatchway of the conning tower, eager to get a breath of fresh air after days of confinement.

The sea is calm, so the captain allows a barbecue on deck. Squeezing through the hatch, you feel like you've stepped into a smelly furnace! It's not that it's so hot outside, or that the air is bad. You're just not used to the sun or the natural sea air. Plus, it's so bright! It takes a few minutes to adjust.

High above you is the conning tower, or sail. The tallest part of the sub, it's like a giant fin. On it is the cockpit, a platform where the captain stands. He fights salt spray and wind to watch the sea and issue commands.

If the waves were high, you wouldn't be out here—it's too easy to get washed overboard. But there's nothing to worry about today. All around you sailors stretch out on the "steel beach." Hamburgers sizzle on the grill. A boom box plays. Dolphins frolic in the waves.

Land is close by. You can't wait to get home. But you don't regret a minute of your voyage. It was the most exciting time of your life!